What Do You See?

Seed Learning

clouds

stars

sun

lightning

rainbow

moon

comet

owl

What do you see?

I see the sun.

What do you see?

I see lightning.

What do you see?

I see a rainbow.

What do you see?

I see a comet.

What do you see?

I see the moon.

What do you see?

I see an owl.

Let's learn about India.

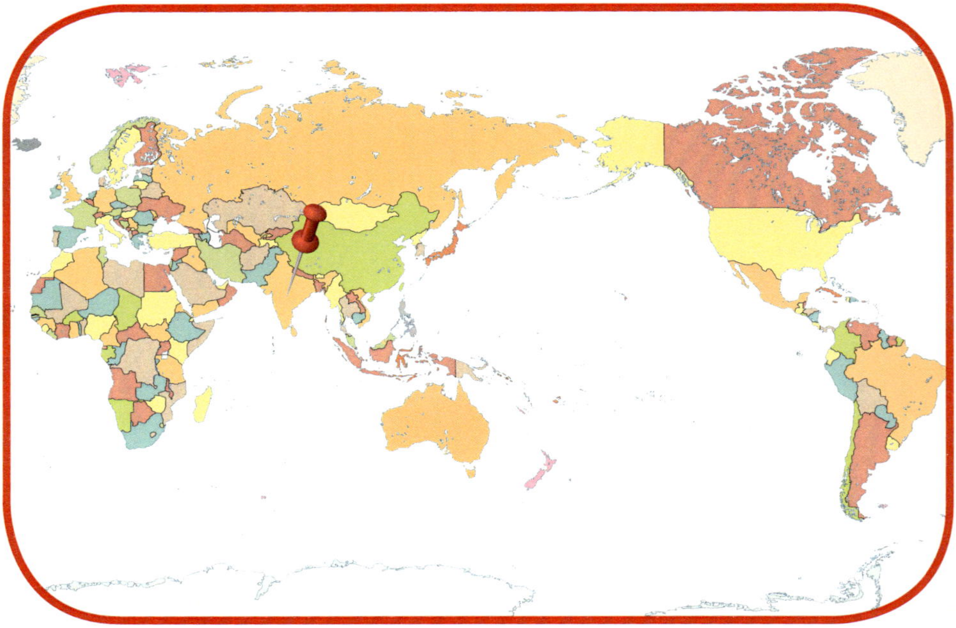

Flag of India

Taj Mahal